THE GRADUATE SURVIVAL GUIDE

5 MISTAKES YOU CAN'T AFFORD TO MAKE IN COLLEGE

"It pays to take life seriously."

PROVERBS 16:20 (The Message)

THE GRADUATE SURVIVAL GUIDE

5 MISTAKES YOU CAN'T AFFORD TO MAKE IN COLLEGE

ANTHONY ONEAL
with Rachel Cruze

RAMSEY
PRESS

This publication is designed to provide accurate and authoritative information with regard to the subject matter covered. It is sold with the understanding that the publisher is not engaged in rendering financial, accounting, or other professional advice. If financial advice or other expert assistance is required, the services of a competent professional should be sought.

Unless noted, all Scripture quotations are taken from the Holy Bible, New Living Translation, copyright ©1996, 2004, 2007, 2013, 2015 by Tyndale House Foundation. Used by permission of Tyndale House Publishers, Inc., Carol Stream, Illinois 60188. All rights reserved.

Scripture quotations from The Message. Copyright © by Eugene H. Peterson 1993, 1994, 1995, 1996, 2000, 2001, 2002. Used by permission of NavPress. All rights reserved. Represented by Tyndale House Publishers, Inc.

Content Development: Rick Prall
Editors: Jen Gingerich, Emma Berry
Cover Design: Tim Newton and Chris Carrico
Interior Design: Tim Newton and Chris Carrico

ISBN: 978-1-9421-2108-4
Printed in the United States of America
17 18 19 20 21 JST 5 4 3 2 1

CONTENTS

ANTHONY ONEAL vi

RACHEL CRUZE x

FOREWORD BY DAVE RAMSEY xii

MISTAKE 01 // STUDENT LOANS 1

MISTAKE 02 // CREDIT CARDS 25

MISTAKE 03 // DUMB CHOICES 45

MISTAKE 04 // NO PLAN 63

MISTAKE 05 // NO MONEY 83

RESOURCES 105

DVD / ONLINE ACCESS .... INSIDE BACK COVER

ANTHONY ONEAL

ANTHONY ONEAL

At age nineteen, Anthony ONeal was deep in debt and short on hope with no direction of where his life was headed. But after hitting rock bottom, Anthony turned his life around and committed himself to helping students find and pursue their passions. Since 2003, Anthony has helped thousands of students succeed with money in their work and personal lives. Now Anthony has joined Ramsey Solutions to spread this encouraging message to students nationwide as a Ramsey Personality.

Before joining Ramsey Solutions, Anthony was the pastor of One Way Youth Ministries at The Bethel Baptist Church in Jacksonville, Florida. It has become one of the fastest growing youth ministries in the country. His youth conferences, concerts, and events have drawn enormous crowds, and he's worked with some of the biggest names in the industry, including Kirk Franklin and Bishop T.D. Jakes' Firehouse Youth Ministry.

You can follow Anthony on Twitter and Instagram at @AnthonyONeal and online at anthonyoneal.com or facebook.com/aoneal.

THE BIGGEST ENEMY TO YOUR SUCCESS IS YOUR EXCUSE!

—ANTHONY ONEAL

RACHEL CRUZE

As a seasoned communicator and Ramsey Personality, Rachel Cruze has been speaking to groups as large as 10,000 for more than a decade. The daughter of Dave Ramsey, she joined Ramsey Solutions in 2010 and uses the knowledge and experiences from growing up in the Ramsey household to educate others on the proper ways to handle their money wisely and stay out of debt. She co-authored the #1 *New York Times* best-selling book *Smart Money Smart Kids* with her dad. Her new book, *Love Your Life, Not Theirs,* released October 2016.

You can follow Rachel on Twitter and Instagram at @RachelCruze and online at rachelcruze.com, youtube.com/rachelcruze, or facebook.com/rachelramseycruze.

A BUDGET HELPS ME LIVE THE LIFE I WANT TO LIVE AND DO THE THINGS I TRULY VALUE.

—RACHEL CRUZE

FOREWORD

DAVE RAMSEY

"Dave! Why in the world don't they teach this stuff in college?"

I had just finished teaching one of my first financial seminars when a lady walked up and hit me with that question. Over the next couple of years, more and more people asked me that same question after live events, at book signings, and on my call-in radio show.

I've heard from millions of people who have completely wrecked their lives by boneheaded money mistakes that started in their college years. I'm a huge fan of education, but I don't think most colleges are really teaching students what they need to know when it comes to handling money wisely.

My broke finance professor told me successful businesses take advantage of sophisticated tools like "other people's money" and "good debt" to really win in the marketplace. I tried that advice after I graduated college—and it led me straight to bankruptcy. I was more than $3 million in debt in my twenties, but I was still following all the financial principles I had learned in school. I'm not always the sharpest tool in the shed, but even I realized something wasn't right.

It took me a long time to clean up that mess and learn how to handle money, and I've spent the last couple of decades helping other people do just that. Now, every day on my radio show, I take calls from people all over the country who have really screwed up their lives because they started depending on debt. And a lot of it is student loan debt and credit card debt that can be traced back to lousy financial decisions they made in college.

Don't let that be you! There are some simple things that—if you learn them early enough, before you get into financial trouble—can completely change the direction of your life. You just need someone to show you how it works.

That's where Anthony ONeal comes in. You'll get to know Anthony—and his story—pretty well in *The Graduate Survival Guide*, but I want you to know two things about him before you even get started: Anthony really hates debt, and Anthony really loves students. I believe you will discover both of those things as you read his stories.

When it comes to debt, he understands just how devastating loans and credit cards can be for a student. He'll tell you all about how he almost wrecked his life with some of the mistakes he made right out of high school.

And when it comes to teaching students, Anthony is one of the most passionate people I've ever met. Before Anthony joined our team at Ramsey Solutions, he led one of the largest student ministries in America. I've discovered that there is nothing that fuels his fire quite like speaking to a room full of teenagers or college students.

If you're headed to college, Anthony will show you how to:

» **Go to college without student loan debt—the greatest financial roadblock for this generation.**

» **Avoid credit cards like the plague.**

» **Take college choices seriously—not just where you go and what you study, but also things like meal plans and housing choices.**

» **Start living on a budget so you can take control of your money.**

» **Focus on saving money now to get a head start on long-term wealth building.**

I'll be honest with you. The stuff you're about to hear is countercultural. The loudest voices in our society will tell you that you can't go to college without debt, that budgets only steal your joy, and that credit cards let you have everything you want right now with no strings attached.

But those are just myths that will bury you for years to come.

We want you to know the truth—and to act on what you know. If you're willing to avoid the five mistakes explained in this book, your life will change forever.

And, best of all, you won't have to call my radio show in crisis mode five or ten years from now. Instead, you'll be calling to tell me how you're winning with money—and in life.

YOU WILL
EITHER LEARN
TO MANAGE
MONEY OR
THE LACK
OF IT WILL
ALWAYS
MANAGE YOU.

—DAVE RAMSEY

STUDENT LOAN

BE DIFI

DEBT IS NORMAL

MISTAKE 01 // STUDENT LOANS

MY BIGGEST MISTAKE IN COLLEGE

I've made some really terrible decisions in my life, but taking out student loans in college has been one of my biggest mistakes. **I found out that paying back student loans always takes more time than you think and costs more money than you want to spend.**

I ended up with more than $25,000 in student loans—and that was after only three semesters of college! What's crazy is that I didn't even need all of that money for school. In fact, I used most of it for stuff that had nothing to do with classes: food, clothes, and nights out with my friends! The money was just too easy to get.

My mind-set at the time was to take advantage of the money from my student loans. I'd been told that as long as I was taking at least one class, I wouldn't have to pay the loans back. **(By the way: That's a terrible plan!)**

After getting out of college, however, **my first student loan bill came in the mail . . . for $532!** For one month! At the time, I was only making $800 every two weeks. That meant the bill ate up almost 70% of one paycheck. I realized that I couldn't pay my loan bill and still afford to live and eat—so I just didn't pay it.

The bill eventually went into collections. After the collection people got in touch with me, they took a look at my income and realized there was no way I was going to be able to pay $532 a month. So, they cut my monthly payment down to $135.

While that was an easier payment to make, it also meant I was barely paying the interest portion of my loans. There was no way I'd ever pay off my debt at that rate. Something had to change. **I attacked the debt and paid it off as fast as possible.** At one point, I was sending almost $2,000 a month toward my student loan debt! I wanted that monster dead!

> *Paying back student loans always takes more time than you think and costs more money than you want to spend.*

The bad decisions I made in college wrecked my financial life for years. I was a grown man with a job, but I was still paying for all those stupid nights out with my college friends. That's really not a good way to start your career.

Listen, I get it. When you're in college, you don't want to stop and think about what your finances will look like years down the road. But that mentality keeps you from thinking through all the problems a load of student loan debt can cause.

Take it from someone who's been there: You don't want to end up with a huge pile of student loan debt. **Student loans are the worst financial mistake you can make at this point in your life.** Don't do it!

STUDENT LOANS 101

Most students don't have a clue about what student loans are or why they're such a bad option when it comes to paying for college. When you take student loans, you'll always end up paying a lot more money because of the added interest payments. Interest is the extra money you have to pay for using someone else's money. You can see how it all adds up on pages 7–8.

The bottom line is that any type of student loan (private or federal) is a terrible option for paying your college expenses. You'll have debt, and you'll pay back more money than you borrowed in the first place.

PRIVATE STUDENT LOANS
These loans are funded by a bank, credit union, or school. They typically have higher interest rates, and payments must be made while you are in school. Since these loans are privately funded, you are responsible for all of the interest for the entire life of the loan. Ouch!

FEDERAL STUDENT LOANS
These are the most common types of student loans. They are funded by the federal government and have lower fixed interest rates (the rates stay the same over time). You don't start paying on your loans until six to nine months after you leave school or graduate—the "grace period." *See the chart on page 6 for more details on federal student loans.*

TYPES OF FEDERAL STUDENT LOANS

DIRECT SUBSIDIZED LOANS

Available to undergraduate students with financial need. Your school determines the amount you can borrow. The federal government subsidizes—or pays for—the interest while you're in school and during the grace period, so you aren't responsible for that part. However, when you start making your payments, interest is then added to your loan amount.

DIRECT UNSUBSIDIZED LOANS

Available to undergrads and grad students. There are no financial need requirements. Your school determines the amount you can borrow. The federal government doesn't subsidize—or pay for—the interest on these loans. The interest is added while you're in school and during the grace period. That interest is added to your total loan when you start making payments.

Stafford Loans

These are the most common type of subsidized and unsubsidized loans available with different financial need requirements.

Perkins Loans

These are for students with the greatest financial need and are always subsidized with a lower fixed interest rate.

PLUS Loans

These have a higher fixed interest rate plus a fee for use. There are no loan limits, and interest accumulates during the life of the loan.

- **Parent PLUS** loans are available to parents for their child's college education.
- **Grad PLUS** loans are available to grad students.

PAYING BACK A STUDENT LOAN

If you borrow

$40,000

with the standard student loan terms

6% INTEREST
$444 PER MONTH
10 YEARS OF PAYMENTS

Then you'll pay back

$53,280

(That's **$13,280** more than you borrowed!)

If you borrow

$100,000

with the standard student loan terms

6% INTEREST
$1,100 PER MONTH
10 YEARS OF PAYMENTS

Then you'll pay back

$133,200

(That's **$33,200** more than you borrowed!)

THE DEBT TRAP

RACHEL CRUZE

College can be super expensive!

But—and this is crazy—just by signing their name a few times and accepting some student loans, students can "pay" their whole bill each term in a matter of minutes.

It's so easy, in fact, that a shocking number of students don't even realize they're signing up for loans at all! And those loans will add up. **On average, they total about $40,000 by the time a student graduates from college.**[1] That means as a college graduate, you'll be paying for your college experience for a decade or more!

That's why I encourage students to avoid debt completely— especially student loan debt.

> *Debt is advertised as an easy way to get what you think you need right now.*

Several years ago, I was speaking at a private college and talked to a young guy who was about to graduate with a four-year degree. When I asked him what his plans were for the future, **he said both he and his fiancée had always dreamed of living and working internationally for a nonprofit organization helping those in need.**

Then came the bad news. He told me they each owed $80,000 in student loans. **That meant they would be starting their life together $160,000 in the hole!**

Maybe it's just me, but that's ridiculous!

You can't expect to pay off that kind of debt just by returning the three toasters you get at your wedding shower! I did the math, and the monthly payment for their student loans worked out to about $1,800 per month for ten years.

$1,800 PER MONTH
EVERY SINGLE MONTH
FOR TEN YEARS

I had to break it to them: **Because of their overwhelming student loan debt, they wouldn't be able to pursue their dream of serving internationally any time soon**. That stinks!

The reality is that if they both work full time with average entry-level salaries, **one of them will spend most of their paycheck just to make the student loan payments.** And that's it. Nothing else.

STUDENT LOANS

They can't save that money for a house. They can't use it for a vacation. They can't spend it on new clothes or a night at the movies. And they definitely can't afford to pack up and move to another country to serve others. Their student loan debt completely stole their dream from them.

This is actually a common story with students, and here's the crazy part: **Debt is totally normal in today's culture.** It seems like everyone is taking out student loans.

That couple thought that taking on some debt wasn't a big deal. And most of our country feels the exact same way. **Debt is advertised as an easy way to get what you think you need right now.**

But you don't have to go into debt for college. Trust me, there are plenty of other options, including community college, scholarships, grants, and work-study programs. **Don't let the burden of student loan debt keep you from pursuing your dreams.**

I OWE $60,000.
WITH ALL
THE STUDENT
LOAN PAYMENTS
COMBINED, I PAY
$550 EVERY
MONTH. MY
BIGGEST REGRET
IS THE BURDEN
OF MY STUDENT
LOAN DEBT.

—JESSE M.

YOU CAN GRADUATE WITHOUT ANY DEBT

A COLLEGE STUDENT'S STORY

Before I even learned about Dave Ramsey's financial principles, **I knew I didn't want to experience the stress of student loan debt.** I knew a college education was vital to securing a good job in an extremely competitive market. I didn't want to feel like I had to take the first job that came along just to pay back my student loans; I wanted to be able to focus on the right job for me.

Lots of people told me not to stress about saving money for college because student loans would take care of everything. But that's not what I wanted.

> *I know it may seem impossible, but I'm here to tell you that you can get a college degree without student loan debt!*

I wanted to graduate from college debt-free, so with every side-gig and summer job, I saved 90% of my paycheck— keeping only 10% for spending money. I applied for more than fifty scholarships and was awarded a handful of those, which covered a huge chunk of my tuition.

Amazon was fantastic when it came to textbooks. With their affordable prices, free shipping, and the ability to sell back my books for credit to put toward the next semester's books, **I was able to keep my textbook cost to a minimum.**

I also had some money in savings to help cover my tuition expenses. **I was able to save money by getting a discount when I paid my tuition in full before each semester started.**

Graduating with a four-year degree completely debt-free was extremely liberating! I know it may seem impossible, but **I'm here to tell you that you *can* get a college degree without student loan debt!**

Saving money from work, having support from my mom, and trusting God with my finances were all vital to my success in avoiding student loans. Also, being cost effective and mindful of my spending habits were crucial.

I graduated from college without any debt. Now I have a great job doing something I really enjoy. I can afford to save money and spend it how I choose. That's a great feeling!

. . . .

Carrie Wilson is a recent college graduate.

TUITION PRICING AVERAGES [2]

PRIVATE FOUR-YEAR COLLEGE $32,500 per year

PUBLIC FOUR-YEAR COLLEGE
(out-of-state) $24,000 per year

PUBLIC FOUR-YEAR COLLEGE
(in-state) $9,500 per year

PUBLIC TWO-YEAR COMMUNITY COLLEGE
(in-state) $3,500 per year

$0K $5K $10K $15K

IN-STATE AND COMMUNITY COLLEGES CAN SAVE YOU TONS OF MONEY.

$20K $25K $30K

MONEY FOR COLLEGE

I've told you that student loans will put you in debt for many years and that you'll end up paying more than you need to pay for college. But there are ways to pay for your education without the debt of student loans. Here are a few ideas:

SCHOLARSHIPS

Scholarships are great because they are free money that doesn't have to be repaid. There are hundreds of scholarships out there. Just do an internet search for *scholarships* to find out what's available and be prepared to write some essays.

GRANTS

Grants are another form of financial aid that you don't have to pay back. They are funded by schools, organizations, or federal assistance programs. They're based on your financial need and part-time or full-time school status.

WORK-STUDY PROGRAMS

Work-study programs allow students to work part time while attending school. These may be on-campus or off-campus jobs that provide money to help you pay for school.

APPLYING FOR FINANCIAL AID

To apply for any financial aid, you must first complete the annual Free Application for Federal Student Aid (FAFSA) by going to *fafsa.ed.gov*. Your school uses this information to determine your eligibility for financial aid.

COMMUNITY COLLEGE

Going to a community college is a great way to get a college education *and* save some money in the process. Honestly, future employers are more concerned about your final degree than the school name at the top of your diploma. Here are some benefits of community college:

» **Lower tuition costs**

» **Smaller campus size**

» **Save money by living at home**

» **Flexible class scheduling**

» **Expanded online class opportunities**

» **Variety of programs**

» **Use of the latest technologies**

» **Complete your basic requirement classes**

» **Time to think about what you want to do**

» **Boost your GPA**

» **Specialize in a field of study**

» **Transfer your credits to a university**

DROPPING OUT CAN BE EXPENSIVE

So, what happens to your student loans if you drop out of college? Do they just go away? Nope.

In fact, when you drop out of college, you could end up owing even more money. Depending on when you drop out and the specific policies at your school, you'll still have to pay back the money. Be sure to check into refund deadlines and the cutoff for dropping classes before you make any decisions.

For example, after dropping out, you may have to pay back a portion of your student loan in addition to the cost of your tuition. **You also might even have to pay back a portion of any grant money you received.** Ouch!

Each school has its own financial rules and policies, so you'll need to check into all of that before you make the decision to leave.

Also, don't forget that dropping out starts your six- or nine-month student loan grace period. And while you won't receive a student loan bill right away, the portion of tuition you owe the school will probably be due immediately.

You may also lose eligibility for any scholarships or grants you've been awarded if you decide to return to school in the future. Before dropping out, take a really close look at all of the variables and options. If it's a financial decision, you could consider part-time enrollment and pick up a side job. Try to finish the semester so you can at least transfer some credits.

If your school just isn't right for you, check into options for transferring to another school. If it's a social decision, try getting involved in some on- or off-campus organizations.

Finally—and this is really important—**federal student loans are NOT bankruptable.** That means you can't file bankruptcy to avoid paying back student loans. No matter what, you will still have to pay back your student loans. They won't go away.

71%

of students who drop out of college say it's because it costs too much and/or because they need to work.[3]

THE $21,000 PAYOFF

I didn't know what I was getting into when I signed on the dotted line for school loans. I was the perfect high school student—a solid 4.0 GPA and high scores on the ACT. I even had a scholarship and several grants to go to college.

But when my family's income increased, the grants disappeared. **I didn't qualify anymore—and we didn't have any savings earmarked for my college education.** Suddenly, college was going to cost *me* a lot of money! My school was already expensive, but it felt different when I didn't actually have to come up with the money for tuition.

Knowing what I know now, I would've gotten a job or spent more time filling out scholarship applications. But I didn't. I marched down to the financial aid office, filled out some student loan paperwork, and suddenly had a full bank account. **I paid my tuition and didn't even think twice about the ball and chain I'd just attached to my ankle.**

Then I signed that dotted line again. And again. It was way too easy. **With five student loans, I found myself $21,000 in debt!** But no big deal, because I was still in school and I didn't need to make any payments. Yet.

But everything comes full circle.

My first job out of college paid $28,000 a year, but **it wasn't really enough to make ends meet.** On top of my regular living expenses, I had a horse—and they aren't cheap! I was constantly on edge, always worrying if I would have enough to pay for my horse's board *and* my groceries.

Then came the call: It was time to start paying on my loans. **My stomach dropped. I couldn't afford another monthly bill of $300.** I put the loans into forbearance—delaying when I had to start paying—but the interest kept growing.

> *I felt like I'd failed as an adult. I worried about what people would think of me.*

About a year later, the student loan payments kicked back in, and I had no choice but to start paying them. And they hit me hard financially. **I could barely afford to pay my bills and make the minimum payments on my loans.** An unfortunate series of events, including my student loans, forced me to make the uncomfortable decision to move back home.

I had a wonderful relationship with my family, but moving home felt shameful. I felt like I'd failed as an adult. I worried about what people would think of me; I wondered what explanation I would give. **I was miserable for the first few months, usually closing myself off in my room after work.**

When I finally added up how much money I owed, I knew something had to change. If I paid the loans off at the regular rate, it would be a long time before I could travel or have horses again. With that as my main motivation, I started attacking my debt by throwing 70% of my paycheck at my loans. **I saw two big results: The numbers dropped, and I started to shed the shame I felt for moving back home.**

I shaved down my grocery budget. I killed my entertainment spending. Netflix and the gym became my primary hobbies. I turned down dinner invitations. My vacations went from weeks at the beach to long weekends visiting friends for free.

It took eleven months of sacrifice to pay off those loans. **It was a long, uncomfortable, and emotional road.** But I did it.

I can say that it's been the longest year of my life. **I learned a lot about patience, focus, and sacrifice.** I learned how to say no when I really want to say yes—to things like spontaneous trips with friends or buying a new pair of boots when the heel goes out on my trusty old pair. I learned how to sit in the discomfort now to be able to do those things later.

I'm not sure what my life would have looked like if I didn't have loans. I think I would've jumped at the chance to travel. I would have gone on more mission trips. I'd have enough money to put a nice down payment on a house. **If I could have a do-over, I would never sign up for school loans. I'd hunt for every other alternative and avoid the mess I created for myself.**

. . . .

Kayla Bates is a recent college graduate.

KNOWING WHAT
I KNOW NOW,
I WOULD NEVER
SIGN UP FOR
STUDENT LOANS.
IT WAS ONE OF
THE BIGGEST
MISTAKES OF
MY LIFE.

—KAYLA B.

02

MISTAKE 02 // CREDIT CARDS

THEY GOT ME WITH "FREE" STUFF!

The first day I arrived at my college, I was so excited to check everything out! As I made my way across campus, I noticed tables set up in long rows. At the tables were representatives from banks, credit card companies, stores, car companies, and many other businesses.

One guy caught my attention and asked, **"Would you like two free large pizzas and a free T-shirt?"**

I was brand-new at college and thought, *Two free pizzas? I love pizza, and who doesn't want a free T-shirt?* When I said yes, he told me all I had to do was *apply* for a credit card. **I knew there was no way I was going to get approved, so I applied.** He got me with the "free" stuff.

That was day one of my first week at college. The credit card companies got my attention with food and clothes—the types of things college students want and need.

Then, the credit card came in the mail. It was so cool! I felt like an adult! My mom, however, wasn't so excited. My mail was still going to her house, and she saw the envelope from the credit card company. She warned me, "Anthony, you don't need that credit card."

I told her, "Hey, I'm eighteen years old. I'm ready for more responsibility. I've got this." I took my new credit card, and I called my girlfriend. I said, "Hey, I've got some money. Where do you want to go for dinner?" We went to a lobster house and ate and ate. We ordered all the crab, lobster—everything. The bill, for two people, was $150!

The next morning, I ordered more stuff for her: roses, two boxes of chocolates, and a teddy bear. That was another $150. Then I went to the mall and bought her a fancy, expensive, name-brand purse for $160. I spent the last bit of money putting gas in my car to go see her.

Within the first eighteen hours, I had maxed out the $500 limit on my new credit card. Actually, I burned through it like it was nothing. And it didn't even bother me.

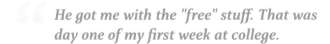

He got me with the "free" stuff. That was day one of my first week at college.

Then the first bill came with a minimum payment of $15. I couldn't believe it! I only had to pay $15 every month for all the stuff I bought. That was fantastic . . . and cheap. **But I told myself I would never use that credit card again.**

A month later, the second statement came. The bank included a note that said something like, "Thank you for making your first payment on time. We see that you could use a larger credit limit, so we are pleased to let you know your spending limit is now $1,000."

I was approved to spend another $500! So that same day, I used my credit card and put a $500 sound system in the back of my 1987 Nissan Maxima—a car that wouldn't even go into reverse. **In just one hour, I maxed out my credit card again!**

When I saw how easy it was to get and use credit cards, I started applying everywhere. I wanted more. It was like I couldn't get enough of them—and the ability to buy stuff.

I ended up with seven credit cards. **I also ended up with more than $15,000 dollars of credit card debt**—and that was on top of all the student loans I had already taken out. To make things even worse, I went and financed thousands of dollars of furniture!

It's crazy how much debt I racked up. **I bought into the lie that buying stuff on credit is the way to go.** But all I ended up with was a ton of debt that took me years to pay off, and I missed out on enjoying things in my present.

The moral of my story is that there's no such thing as a free T-shirt. In fact, that T-shirt ended up costing me over $1,000 in just the first few months. There's no T-shirt that's worth that much money!

DEBT IS DUMB. CASH IS KING. DEBT IS NORMAL. BE WEIRD.

—DAVE RAMSEY

DON'T FALL FOR THESE DEBT MYTHS

For decades, people have believed the only way to really enjoy life is to rack up piles of debt. Wrong. You can live without the burden of debt payments. Just be careful that you don't fall for these five myths about debt and credit.

MYTH: YOU NEED TO HAVE A CREDIT CARD.

Truth: A debit card will do everything a credit card will do—except put you in debt. The best part of using a debit card is that you're only spending money you already have in the bank.

MYTH: CAR PAYMENTS ARE A WAY OF LIFE.

Truth: Car payments will keep you in debt the rest of your life. Buy a cheap used car with cash, save money for a car every month, and upgrade when you can. Repeat that process. You'll end up driving nice (used) cars and never have to use debt to do it.

MYTH: CREDIT IS FUN BECAUSE I CAN BUY WHATEVER I WANT.

Truth: Debt is anything *but* fun—in fact, it's no fun at all. Your monthly debt payments will eat up most of your income and keep you from enjoying other things in life.

MYTH: A CREDIT CARD IS GOOD TO HAVE IN CASE OF EMERGENCIES.

Truth: Having at least $500 cash in the bank—an emergency fund—is the best idea for handling life's emergencies. Cash is always the best option. The last thing you need in an emergency is to go into debt.

MYTH: CREDIT CARD REWARD PROGRAMS ARE A GREAT BENEFIT.

Truth: Most people spend more with a credit card than they would with cash, and most reward points go unused. Any perks you do earn are wiped away by the extra spending, interest payments, and fees.

CREDIT CARDS

CREDIT

- BORROW AND SPEND MONEY YOU DON'T HAVE
- PAY INTEREST ON MONEY YOU DON'T HAVE
- BUY AIRLINE TICKETS, RESERVE HOTELS, RENT A CAR
- PURCHASE AND FRAUD PROTECTION
- OFTEN AN ANNUAL FEE
- RACKS UP DEBT

DEBIT

SPEND MONEY YOU ALREADY HAVE

NO INTEREST, NO PAYMENTS

BUY AIRLINE TICKETS, RESERVE HOTELS, RENT A CAR

PURCHASE AND FRAUD PROTECTION

GENERALLY FREE TO USE

DEBT-FREE SPENDING

THE TRUTH ABOUT CREDIT SCORES

When most people think of a credit score, they often think of the FICO score because that's the one you hear mentioned on TV. The FICO score, named after the company that computes credit scores, is just one of the ways credit scores are measured. Other companies, such as Equifax, Transunion, and Experian, also compute credit scores.

Here's the shocker: According to FICO's website, 100% of your score is based on your *debt*, not your wealth. It has nothing to do with your savings, your income, or your investments.

What's really amazing is that you could inherit $1 million tomorrow from some relative and it would not change your credit score one bit—even though you'd be a millionaire!

The credit score is not a measure of winning financially. A high credit score just means that you have debt, use debt, and love debt. **At the end of the day, the FICO score is just an "I love debt" score.**

COMPONENTS OF A FICO SCORE[4]

10% TYPE OF DEBT

10% NEW DEBT

15% DURATION OF DEBT

30% DEBT LEVEL

35% DEBT PAYMENT HISTORY

BUY YOURSELF A CAR WITH CASH

You may think you need to buy a brand-new car—and you need a loan to do it. **But that's the most expensive way to buy a car.** Period.

First of all, that brand-new car will lose a huge chunk of value the moment you drive it off the car lot. Seriously. You could buy a car, pull out of the dealer's lot, drive around the block, and never be able to sell it for what you paid for it ten minutes earlier. Just picture yourself emptying a bag of cash out of the window as you drive off—because that's exactly what's happening.

Do you need a brand-new car? No. What you really need is a vehicle that will get you from one place to another, like to work or class and back.

The problem is that a lot of us value what people think about us based on the car we drive. **We think driving a certain type of car makes us a better person.**

That's pretty messed up when you think about it.

Your value as a person is not measured by the type of car you drive. And you certainly don't need a monthly car payment. The average car loan payment is almost $500 every month.[5] That's crazy!

Here's a plan. Take the bus or get a ride from a friend. Save up $1,000 or $2,000 and buy a used car that will get you around.

Of course, you'll want to have liability insurance and enough money for gas and to keep your car running.

Then, every month, you can basically pay *yourself* that car payment that everyone else is sending to the bank. Put some cash in your savings account every month specifically earmarked for a car. **If you save $250 per month for a year, you would have $3,000 to apply toward another car.**

If you sold your current car for $1,000, you would have **$4,000 to upgrade your car after just one year.**

If you kept saving, a year later you would have another $3,000. Add that to the sale of your $4,000 car and you could afford a nicer car after just two years.

The key is saving car payments for yourself rather than paying them to someone else with interest. And don't tell me you can't afford to save a few hundred dollars a month if you're *already* thinking about getting a car loan! If it's going to hit your monthly budget anyway, skip the bank and new-car depreciation and choose to drive debt-free.

CREDIT CARDS

MARKETING WORKS

There are many different things you can buy—but you only have so much money. That means you can't buy everything, even if you wanted to.

Companies know this. So, they spend a lot of money on marketing, and they study the spending habits of college students. Based on the results, companies will create TV, radio, and even social media ads targeted directly to you. **Some research indicates that the average American is exposed to over 4,000 advertisements every day.**[6]

Now, advertising and marketing aren't evil, but you do have to be careful. The most effective ads target your wants and needs and make you feel as though companies really care about you. However, most of those companies are just trying to get you to buy their stuff.

Marketing is all around you. Names, logos, and labels are on everything. You probably have several logos within eyeshot right now. These names and labels generate brand loyalty— and that's why so much money is spent on advertising.

Companies also spend a lot of money buying the best shelf spaces at your favorite stores. And they pay for product placement so that specific brands show up in the hands of your favorite actors in your favorite movies. The results of marketing can be seen in the things we buy.

HOW COLLEGE STUDENTS SPEND THEIR MONEY

According to a recent survey of college students,[7] here is how they spend their money (beyond tuition, room, and board):

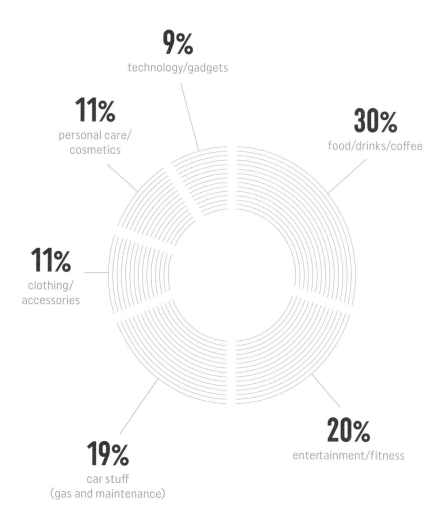

9%
technology/gadgets

11%
personal care/
cosmetics

11%
clothing/
accessories

30%
food/drinks/coffee

20%
entertainment/fitness

19%
car stuff
(gas and maintenance)

MESSED UP BY DEBT

Debt can definitely mess up your life when it comes to your personal finances. **It took me years to clean up the mess that I'd created.** I felt like I couldn't do what I wanted to do with my money—because I was constantly sending it out to pay back all of my debt.

I spent a lot of time after college paying for the mistakes I made in my past while I was in school. **Between student loans and credit card spending, I had over $40,000 of debt.**

That debt derailed my life for years. It's true what the biblical proverb says—the borrower is slave to the lender (Proverbs 22:7). But it doesn't have to be that way! You can avoid making the same mess of your finances that I did.

> *Debt slowed down my dreams. I spent too much time paying for my past instead of enjoying my present and planning for my future.*

My sister is one example of someone who did it right. She saw what I went through because of my terrible financial choices. As a result, she never went down the road of debt. I'm so thankful she never took out student loans and she didn't sign up for any credit cards while she was in college. In fact, at the age of twenty-five, the only debt she has is her mortgage payment! That's awesome!

I know how much debt can hurt your life. I wish I'd learned to make wise decisions with my money earlier. If I'd had a dream for my life and stuck to a plan, I would be in a much better place financially. I could be living in a nice house and driving my dream car debt-free. And I should have a bunch of money saved in the bank, but I don't.

Debt slowed down my dreams. I spent too much time paying for my past instead of enjoying my present and planning for my future. Now that I have a better understanding of the right way to take care of my money, I have a dream and a plan to get there. I'm back on track financially. **I just wish I hadn't wasted all those years being in debt.**

87%

of college student spending is done with cash, debit cards, or prepaid cards.[8]

COLD, HARD CASH

When it comes to finances, my mother has a saying that continues to run through my mind even today: **"Don't buy something you can't afford. If you don't have the money to purchase it, don't buy it."**

All through high school and my freshman year of college, every time I wanted to buy something I would first go to the bank and get cash. **Only when I had the money—in cold, hard cash—would I pay for something.** There were situations where I ended up not buying certain items because the things weren't worth the cost compared to the cash.

As a sophomore in college, I started using a debit card for some purchases. Using my debit card made my life a lot easier—and in certain situations, safer—since I wasn't carrying around stacks of money all the time.

I graduated from college completely debt-free—no student loans and no credit cards. The key to my success was living within my means and sticking to a plan. **I treated every purchase and swipe as if I was handing over the money in cold, hard cash.**

. . . .

Jack Singleton is a recent college graduate.

I'VE NEVER OWNED A CREDIT CARD. PAYING IN CASH GIVES ME A VISUAL OF AN ITEM'S VALUE.

—JOHN S.

MORROW

MISTAKE 03 // DUMB CHOICES

MAKE SMART CHOICES

When I went to college, I was faced with so many different choices. To be honest, it was all a bit overwhelming.

I've already told you about some of my terrible choices related to student loans and credit cards. And then there were the dumb decisions in how I spent my money—like spending a bunch on a car that couldn't even go in reverse.

But I also made bad choices when it came to school. **I chose to not go to class because I wanted to hang out with friends.** I didn't study or take work seriously—and I didn't give a lot of thought to a major or what I wanted to do as a career.

If you're not careful, some of your decisions can really hurt you. For example, I know a young lady who started college with a **full-ride scholarship that covered everything:** dorm, meals, tuition—everything. She was set!

Now, you *know* college life includes parties, right? Well, while she was at a party one night, **someone took a video of her dancing on a table.** She thought it was pretty funny, so she posted the video on social media for all of her friends to see. Pretty normal stuff, right?

The very next day, she lost her scholarship. All of it.

Why? Because someone from the school saw the video. They determined it was inappropriate and put the school in a bad light. So this young lady, who had worked her tail off, had to leave school because she could no longer afford the tuition.

This is *so* important. **Be careful with what you post online.** Don't make the same mistake she made.

EVERY DECISION, EVERY CHOICE, EVERY POST BECOMES
A PART OF YOUR DIGITAL IMPRINT FOR THE
ENTIRE WORLD TO SEE.

When you post something, don't assume it's private or you can just delete it later. What you post online today could be your biggest regret in a few years when you're looking for a job—or even a spouse. Every decision, every choice, every post becomes a part of your digital imprint for the entire world to see.

It's *that* serious. Just stop and think. Take all of your choices seriously. Don't make a snap decision that you'll regret for years to come. **Remember, your future depends on the choice—that ONE choice—you make today.**

CHOOSING A MAJOR

Some students go to college knowing exactly what they want to do for a career. Many, however, enter college undecided about a major. That's okay. The reality is that many students change their major during the first two years. You'll be taking a lot of basic classes during that time anyway. And there's nothing wrong with changing your major.

But locking in a major by the end of your first or second year is a big deal because it will determine a majority of the classes you will need to take from then on. It really is one of those "it's that serious" type of choices. Here are five ideas to help you choose your major:

CONSIDER YOUR INTERESTS AND PASSIONS

What do you really enjoy? What's your passion? What topics or subjects interest you? If your major is something you really enjoy, you'll be more likely to study and go to class.

EXPLORE SOME OPTIONS

If you aren't sure what you want to study, list "Undeclared" as your major. That won't lock you into any set plan. During your first few semesters, try several fields of study to see what clicks. Get input from other students and guidance counselors, too.

CONSIDER THE COST RATIO

Don't spend $100,000 getting a degree for a job that will only pay you $32,000 per year. But don't let a salary be the only factor in choosing your career. Keep in mind that no amount of money can make you enjoy a job you absolutely hate!

EXAMINE THE JOB OPTIONS

Make sure there are jobs in demand for the major you choose. Also, a major that provides several options is better than a major that only gives you one career choice. You don't want to spend four years in school and then not be able to get a job.

SHADOW SOMEONE FOR A DAY

Follow someone in your intended career field for a day or two to see what kinds of things they do—and if you would enjoy it. It's better to find out what you like or don't like before you get too far down the requirements for your major.

Don't rush your decision. Spend some time discovering what will be your best choice for a major. Don't pick a major just because your best friend did or because you can make a bunch of money once you graduate and have a career. Your major should be a reflection of who you are and what interests you.

DUMB CHOICES

PURCHASE WISELY

When it's time to make a purchase, especially a large one, always stop and think about it. Seriously. Take a breath. **Don't give in to impulse purchases**—seeing something you think you can't live without and buying it right then and there.

I've found that it's always a good idea to do some research before you make a large purchase. Of course, the internet is a great resource when it comes time to find information. Just remember: **You can't believe everything you read online.**

However, when it comes to product reviews, the internet can be a big help in making wise purchases. Just search for reviews to see what others have to say. Be careful, though, because a lot of what you find online is actually marketing disguised as product reviews. **Find a few reputable sources you like and stick to them.**

Beyond official product reviews, you also want to see what actual owners have to say about whatever you're interested in. Surveys indicate that over half of us consider what other people say about products on social media and **70% read online reviews before buying something.**[9]

As long as you look on reputable sites, you should be able to find reviews you can use to make decisions. If you don't feel comfortable about a product after reading what actual owners of that product think, don't buy it.

Another great thing I've learned to do is wait a day or two before making a larger purchase. Sometimes we get so excited about buying something that we rush into a dumb decision. You can usually avoid that by waiting overnight. If it still seems like a good idea the next day and you can afford it, go for it.

Finally, make sure you can pay cash for the purchase. One of my favorite sayings is, "Don't desire the latest; desire the greatest." When it comes to making purchases, the greatest purchase is a debt-free purchase. It's always a bad idea to go into debt for a purchase.

Here's one last piece of advice: **If you don't have the cash, you can't afford it.**

84%

of people have made
an impulse purchase at
some time.[10]

BEWARE OF SCAMS

RACHEL CRUZE

As a college student, you're a prime target for scammers trying to steal your money, your personal information, and even your identity. You have to be careful.

A recent study indicates that more than 22% of identity theft and fraud cases happen to college students.[11] However, the same study reports that 64% of college students said they were not very concerned about fraud. That means two out of three college students aren't worried about it, even though it happens to one out of every five students! Wake up!

My sister, Denise, had a terrible experience with a money scam. **During her first week at college, she got an email that she thought had come from the university administration offices.** It certainly looked legitimate. The email said something like this:

> Notice: Your tuition for this semester has not been paid in full. Immediate action is required if you desire to stay in your classes. Please use the university link below to enter you bank account information to complete the payment on your account. Reminder: This is time-sensitive information; your immediate attention is required to avoid academic suspension. If you fail to respond, you will no longer be enrolled in the university.

Naturally, Denise freaked out and clicked on the link to enter her bank account information. After paying the money that the site said she owed, Denise headed to class.

The next day, she checked her bank account to make sure the tuition had been paid. **To her surprise—and horror—her entire bank account had been cleaned out.** It was all a scam! She was the victim of fraud.

> *As a college student, you're a prime target for scammers trying to steal your money.*

Every year, these types of scams target inexperienced and naïve students who are entering college. So, what should you do if you get that kind of email?

First, talk with the school office to check the validity of the email. They'll tell you if it's genuine. However, rather than sending an email asking for this information, the school will ask you to come into the office to pay in person. **Legitimate businesses, universities, colleges, and government offices will never ask you for your bank account information or other sensitive personal information in an email.**

Don't provide access to your bank account to anyone unless you're sure of who it is and why they need your information. **Also, when it comes to scams, remember this: If it sounds too good to be true, it probably is!**

WAYS TO SAVE CASH

Going away to college can be exciting—but it can be expensive, too. With some planning and creativity, you may be able to save some money in the following areas:

ROOM AND BOARD

This has to do with where you're going to live and what you're going to eat. The average cost for room and board, depending on where you go to college, can range from $9,000 to $12,000 per year.[12]

Housing: Some colleges require freshmen to live on campus. You won't have to look for a place to live, but on-campus housing may be more expensive. Living off campus may allow you to save money if you split the rent with roommates.

Another budget-friendly way to handle room and board— after your freshman year—is to be a resident assistant (RA). At most schools, RAs enjoy free or reduced rooming costs and even some meals in exchange for their work.

Eating: Most colleges require freshmen to purchase a meal plan. Research your options. Be realistic with the amount of meals you'll eat per week. For example, if you typically just grab a piece of fruit or a granola bar for breakfast, it would be cheaper to buy those at the store and not pay for the extra meals on a meal plan. At most schools, you can't roll unused meals to the next semester, so you could end up wasting a lot of money on unused meals. Also pay attention to how much money you spend eating out off campus.

If you live off campus, you can save money by preparing your meals at home. Pack a lunch and snacks to take to class with you. A brown bag in your backpack won't ruin your image!

BOOKS

Another major cost each semester will be the books for your classes. Books are really overpriced, and you don't have a choice about whether or not to buy them. The average cost of books and supplies is around $1,200 per year.[13] You can save money by purchasing used books or e-books, borrowing books, buying them online, or even renting your books.

ENTERTAINMENT

Rather than spending a fortune on a fancy gym membership or going out to eat, check out campus options. You can borrow movies from the library, use the campus gym, play intramural sports, and get involved in all kinds of clubs and organizations. Colleges usually have a monthly list of campus activities, and most of them should be fairly cheap.

$85

The average cost of a college textbook:[14]
(Some textbooks have $200–400 price tags!)

REAL-LIFE WISDOM

Before you know it, you'll wake up and be twenty-five years old. Don't become that person who looks back on their college days with a pile of regret because of the decisions they made while in school.

Every decision you make today will have consequences—positive or negative—on your future. Here are some choices and wisdom you'll be thankful for several years from now.

BUILD QUALITY RELATIONSHIPS
A handful of really good friends will become more important than a bunch of mediocre relationships.

STAY OUT OF DEBT
Your post-college budget will thank you for not having a mountain of debt payments that eat up your paycheck.

PURSUE YOUR PASSIONS
Turning your passions into a paying career is always a bonus. You'll make money and enjoy what you're doing.

UNDERSTAND THE IMPORTANCE OF INSURANCE
Renter's, health, and auto insurances will protect you and your money. Sure, they cost money, but if you ever need them, you'll be glad you have them.

EMBRACE CHANGE

No matter how good or bad things may be, you can always count on change. Being able to adapt to change will help you in the long run.

RECOGNIZE THE POWER OF COMPOUND INTEREST

Compound interest is amazing and helps you build wealth! When you save (or invest), compound interest is added to your principal amount and to the previous interest you've earned—year after year. Compound interest needs two things to make you a millionaire: money invested and time to grow. So, start investing as early as you can!

BELIEVE IN YOURSELF

Have confidence in yourself and what you can do. Don't let anyone else tell you who or what you should be.

BE CAUTIOUS ONLINE

Anything you post online becomes part of your digital footprint. Things online live forever, so be smart with what you post. It will follow you everywhere.

TAKE CARE OF YOURSELF

If healthy eating and exercise aren't a normal part of your life already, now is the perfect time to make that change. You'll not only create good habits that will keep you strong and healthy for life, but you'll also have more energy to do the things you want to do today.

DUMB CHOICES

STAY FOCUSED

I wasn't worried about my grades in college. I was more concerned about my girlfriend, my friends, my fraternity, dancing with my step troupe—stuff like that. **I just wanted to be popular.** I was more focused on extracurricular things than schoolwork.

To be honest, going to my classes and studying were not high on my priority list. **I didn't take my choices seriously, and I ended up in a huge financial mess.**

I wish I could go back and tell my eighteen-year-old self, "This is serious! Make better choices, focus on school, and stay out of debt!" I wish this because decisions I made back then ended up costing me years of trouble and thousands of dollars. It was hard to start my life and plan for my future while I was still paying for all of the dumb choices I made in college—with both my money and my priorities.

You have to focus. Focus on your education. Focus on getting it debt-free. Zone in. And yeah, this means you may not be able to do some of the things your friends are doing, but you've got to do what works for you in the long run.

In several years, your friends may be $50,000 in debt and working jobs they hate just to pay their bills. If you focus and take your decisions seriously now, you can jump into your adult life without being weighed down by old mistakes.

Here's one of my favorite quotes that challenges me to stay focused: **The caliber of your future will be determined by the choices you make today!** That just means the choices you make now will determine if you will be successful tomorrow, next week, and even into the future.

> *I wish I could go back and tell my eighteen-year-old self, "This is serious! Make better choices!"*

With an "it's that serious" mind-set, you can begin to do the things that really matter. You can do the things that will make a positive impact on your future. **Take college—and all the decisions you make—seriously. This stuff matters!**

68%

of college students binge-watch television shows on Netflix (watching three or more shows in a row).[15]

THE REAL WORLD

In my first semester, I was too focused on friends and my social life—and not focused enough on school. I ended up failing that semester. It took a lot of hard work to get my GPA up from a 1.0 to the 3.6 I graduated with. —Alison B.

My biggest regret was my time management skills. I also wish I had been more proactive with my assignments. —Daniel W.

I remember the monumental anxiety I had over so many things: class registration, essay due dates, finals, and other stuff. If I'd taken it all seriously, I would have had an easier time managing the stress levels. —Rebecca J.

The most significant regret I have is the major I chose. I didn't have adequate information at the age of eighteen to make an intelligent decision about my career path. —Colby M.

I wish someone had told me to keep in touch with the best friends you meet in college. Life will take you in different directions. I wish I had known to cherish those friendships when they were with me. —Kristen M.

The most helpful advice I received was to get involved in campus organizations. I got to take on leadership roles and really come out of my shell. —Melissa W.

I WISH I WOULD'VE KNOWN THAT COLLEGE WASN'T GOING TO BE LIKE HIGH SCHOOL. IT REQUIRED A LOT MORE RESPONSIBILITY THAN I EXPECTED.

—ROBERT P.

DON'T FAKE IT

MAKE

'TIL YOU

IT

04

MISTAKE 04 // NO PLAN

LIVING ON A BUDGET

I didn't realize the importance of a budget until I found myself living paycheck to paycheck. I had been out of school for six months, and the grace period for my student loans was over. When I opened my first loan bill, I was shocked at the amount—and didn't know what I was going to do!

I was working and earning money, but I had no idea how to balance my income and my expenses. I never knew how much money I had or when the next bill was coming. **I was living without a plan for my money, and I was going crazy trying to juggle everything.**

My dad saw me struggling with my money, so he sat me down and showed me how to do a budget. He spent time teaching me some things about how money works and how to create a plan for my income and expenses.

Getting on a budget was the best decision I ever made with money. It was the step that enabled me to turn my mess around! Now, after a few years of experience, I've found that living on a budget is the best way to reach my dreams.

My budget is like a compass that guides me. A compass is a tool that helps keep you going in the right direction. A budget is a tool that helps you stay on the right path with your money. **When I was younger, I was living without a budget to serve as my compass.**

One of my favorite sayings is an old sailors' proverb: *"He who is enslaved to the compass has freedom to the seas. The rest must sail close to the shore."* To be enslaved to a compass just means that you are locked into following the directions provided by the compass—it's your guide. **That's what a budget does—it guides your money decisions.**

Without a compass, a sailor has to sail close to shore and depend on other things for guidance. My "close to the shore" was not a good place to be. **I based my money decisions on what my peers were doing.**

It was normal to me to rack up debt and live without a budget. I thought I was experiencing life, but I really wasn't. In fact, that debt actually slowed my life down and kept me in financial bondage for years.

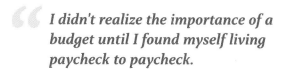

> *I didn't realize the importance of a budget until I found myself living paycheck to paycheck.*

I could be a lot further along in my life if I had made wiser decisions and lived on a budget. **But I didn't take the time to dream, and I didn't have a plan.** I didn't have a plan for my life, and I certainly didn't have a plan for my money.

All the money I made went back out the door to pay my debt. I never seemed to have any extra money to spend on stuff I wanted. For a long time, I was paying for my past instead of enjoying my present and preparing for my future.

Now I'm focused on having a plan for my money. I recognize the guidance a budget provides for my financial decisions—just like a compass provides navigation guidance for a sailor. There's even a proverb that talks about the importance of budgeting: "Good planning and hard work lead to prosperity, but hasty shortcuts lead to poverty" (Proverbs 21:5).

The shortcuts I took—student loans and credit cards—just made a mess of my finances. Now I understand what a budget can do for me. **I take my budget seriously because my money choices can either move me closer toward my dreams or push me back into debt.**

68%

of people do not use a detailed budget, according to a recent Gallup poll.[16]

HE WHO IS
ENSLAVED TO
THE COMPASS
HAS FREEDOM
TO THE SEAS.
THE REST
MUST SAIL
CLOSE TO
THE SHORE.

—OLD SAILORS' PROVERB

HOW TO BUDGET

A budget is just a written plan for your money. It doesn't have to be fancy or complicated. But if you live without a budget, you'll get to the end of the month and have no idea where all your hard-earned money went. **Author John Maxwell puts it simply: "A budget is telling your money where to go instead of wondering where it went."**

To win with money, you need a zero-based budget every month. That just means you're planning out all of your spending ahead of time. You're giving every dollar you earn a job to do. That way, when you write it down, your income minus your expenses equals zero.

Here's how it's done: Start by listing all of your sources of income for the month. This includes paychecks from work or side jobs, financial support from family, and any other money.

Next, list every expense you have for the month. This includes school fees, rent, food, clothing, gas for your car, entertainment—everything! Do this every month, because your budget will change depending on what's going on.

Remember: You're the boss of your budget—until you write it down. Then it's the boss! **Once you've set it, stick to it.** Don't get discouraged if the first month is a little bumpy. It usually takes two or three months to get the hang of it. On the next page you'll see what a sample budget looks like.

BUDGET FOR THIS MONTH

INCOME

Paychecks from work .... $ 800
Support from parents .... $ 200
Odd jobs.. $ 100

Total = $1,100

EXPENSES

Giving... $ 110
Saving for tuition .... $ 500
Books/school supplies .... $ 150
Gas for car... $ 60
Clothes .... $ 80
Entertainment .... $ 80
Eating out .... $ 120

Total = $1,100

TOTAL

Income $1,100
Expenses .... - $1,100

MY FAVORITE TOOL FOR BUDGETING

RACHEL CRUZE

I confess: I'm a free spirit and I love to spend money. For the longest time, budgeting was just something I *had* to do. Unlike the spreadsheet nerds out there, crunching numbers wasn't my idea of fun. Maybe you feel the same way. If so, let me give you a head start on what I've learned.

A budget doesn't *limit* your freedom. A budget actually *gives* you freedom. In fact, having a budget has allowed me to spend money and not feel guilty about it—that's a big win for the spender in me!

The same will be true for you. The sooner you start using a budget, the sooner you'll lose the guilt and actually have cash on hand to spend how you choose.

Knowing that you should use a budget is great, but most of us find it difficult to actually create one. So, when the fantastic company I work for developed a new app that makes budgeting easy, I was *super* excited! **The app is called EveryDollar, and it's by far my favorite budget tool.** Even better, it's free!

Since I'm constantly on the go, I love that my EveryDollar budget is always with me—whether I choose to check it on my smartphone with the EveryDollar app or on my home computer via everydollar.com. Having that visibility is really important when it comes to sticking to your budget.

And since EveryDollar takes care of the math, all I have to do is create my budget before the month begins and then track my spending throughout the month. That's it! The spender in me who used to dread spreadsheets and numbers can honestly say that EveryDollar has not only made budgeting easy, but it's also made it kind of fun!

A BUDGET DOESN'T LIMIT YOUR FREEDOM. A BUDGET ACTUALLY GIVES YOU FREEDOM.

You might be like me and lean toward spending. Or, maybe you're the more disciplined saver. **Either way, my hope is that you experience the freedom that comes from taking control of your money with a budget.** It's a great feeling! And with EveryDollar, budgeting and freedom are within your reach.

NO PLAN

BUDGET-FRIENDLY DATE IDEAS

You don't have to bust your budget—or go into debt—to enjoy a date. With a little bit of effort, you can find discounts or coupons to help lower the costs of some activities. After all, if the purpose of your date is to spend time together and get to know someone, spending a bunch of money to have a good time doesn't make much sense.

To help you out, here's a list of twenty fun date ideas that are either free or won't cost you a lot of money. Try one of these or explore some other options.

1. **Find a nearby town or city to visit and explore.**

2. **Go for a bike ride together.**

3. **Watch a movie on a laptop/tablet with a picnic lunch.**

4. **Hang some hammocks and enjoy relaxing and talking.**

5. **Cook a meal together and then go out for dessert.**

6. **Explore a nearby state or national park.**

7. **Go geocaching using an app on your smartphone.**

8. **Watch or play intramural sports together.**

9. **Volunteer at a homeless shelter.**

10. Look for free local events at parks or museums.

11. Find discount tickets to a botanical garden or zoo.

12. Check out cars at a classic car show.

13. Go bowling, play mini golf, or toss a Frisbee.

14. Exercise together at a rec center.

15. Go for a hike and take pictures of nature.

16. See a movie at a discount theater.

17. Read and discuss a book together.

18. Visit a local farmers' market, orchard, or flea market.

19. Plan a day at the beach or the lake.

20. Tailgate at a college football game.

The average cost of a dinner-and-movie date:[17]

$90

INSURANCE MATTERS

Let's take a few minutes to talk about insurance, because having the right kinds of insurance really does matter. **You need to make room in your budget for insurance.** Nobody likes talking about insurance because we feel like we pay a bunch of money for something we don't really need. It almost feels like we're wasting money.

But you need to think of insurance as paying a company to take on financial risk instead of you having to do it. **You pay a small monthly insurance premium to a company that agrees to pay for a large financial loss if it occurs.** Basically, you're paying for a layer of protection that will take the hit for you if or when something bad, like a car accident, happens.

Here's an example: When I was in college, I went out the front door one morning to head to the gym. But when I got outside, I couldn't find my car. It wasn't where I left it. It was gone! **Someone stole my car! I couldn't believe it!**

I almost had a heart attack, but thankfully I had insurance. When the police finally found my car, it needed over $9,000 in repairs. I sure didn't have that much money to fix my car, but my insurance company did.

I had to pay the deductible, which is the money that comes out of your pocket if you have an accident, but the insurance company covered the rest.

So what kind of insurance do you need right now? While you're in college, there are three basic types of insurance you should absolutely have in place. You may already have these through your parents' insurance policies, but don't assume so. Talk with them about what they cover for you, and then make sure you pick up any that are left.

HEALTH INSURANCE

Health insurance is expensive, but it's necessary. Nobody plans to get sick or have an accident—but it happens. Medical insurance helps pay for your doctor visits, prescriptions, and hospital expenses. If you go to the emergency room without insurance, you'll find out what "expensive" *really* means!

AUTO INSURANCE

If you drive a car, you need auto insurance. There are two kinds: liability and collision. You really need them both. Liability insurance pays to repair or replace someone else's property and covers others' medical costs if you cause an accident. Collision coverage pays to repair or replace your car if you're in an accident that you caused or if you get hit by an uninsured driver.

RENTER'S INSURANCE

Renter's insurance (or contents insurance) covers your stuff if it's stolen or damaged. If you're living in a dorm at school, your parents' homeowner's insurance should cover your stuff. However, if you're renting an apartment or house off campus, you definitely need renter's insurance. The good news is that it's super cheap, usually less than $20 per month.

MAKING MONEY

If the "poor college student" lifestyle is a reality for you, then finding some ways to make extra money may be at the top of your to-do list. The best way to make money is by going to work. Yes, work. A recent study showed that about 70% of college students work twenty to thirty hours per week.[18]

Now that may not be the life you always dreamed of having in college, but it's reality. Life costs money, and money comes from work!

A good place to start when looking for work is the student employment office on campus. Colleges and universities depend on students for many jobs that would otherwise require a full-time salaried position. You can make money working for your school, like in the bookstore or doing basic administrative work.

Of course, a campus job is just one way to earn extra income while you're in school. Here are some other ideas:

MAKE MONEY ONLINE
If you already have a blog or video channel, putting small ads on your site will help monetize your online efforts every time someone checks out your stuff. Just don't invest a ton of money into any kind of crazy get-rich-quick internet scam. The goal is to *make* money, not *waste* money!

MAKE AND SELL CRAFTS

If you're crafty, you can make stuff in your spare time and sell it locally at flea markets or craft shows. You can also sell your items on online craft sites.

APPLY FOR SCHOLARSHIPS

Every year, billions of dollars in scholarship and grant money go unclaimed. Spending your extra hours applying for scholarships can become a profitable part-time job. Sure, you have to write some essays, but it can be worth your time.

DO ODD JOBS

There are a bunch of ways to make money if you are willing to put some effort into it—and ask for work. You can mow yards, rake leaves, clean pools, walk dogs, house or pet sit, go grocery shopping for the elderly, or help people move.

COMPLETE ONLINE SURVEYS

A bunch of companies will pay you to take surveys, watch videos, test websites, or review items online.

OFFER TUTORING

Tutor kids in subjects that you excelled at in high school. You can also offer music lessons if you play an instrument well.

BECOME A SECRET SHOPPER

You can get paid to do secret shopper work—or at least get reimbursed for a meal for two people at a restaurant. That will definitely help your food budget!

NO PLAN

COMPARISONS AND CONTENTMENT

RACHEL CRUZE

It used to be that "keeping up with the Joneses" was only a problem if you actually *saw* their stuff in person. Today, with our social media apps, our phone screens are little windows into other people's lives. **If we're not careful, those images can lead us into discontentment and comparison living.**

Facebook, Instagram, and Twitter—just to name a few—have brought a lot of value to the world. But there's also a huge negative: **These networks make it easier than ever for us to wish we were living someone else's life.** What I've come to realize is that, when we start comparing ourselves to people we don't know, we're playing a game we'll never win.

 When we start comparing ourselves to people we don't know, we're playing a game we'll never win.

Most of what you see on social media isn't the whole picture. It's a public display of our *best* self. It's an ideal we want to project out into the world. **Life might be miserable on the other side of the camera, but we post the best images with the best looking filter applied.**

When you get caught up in social media comparisons, you're comparing yourself to make-believe. **And whenever you compare yourself to make-believe, your real life will never feel good enough.**

Even though social media is an easy place to compare our lives to others' lives, we can't forget about comparisons in real life and real time. No matter what we do, where we go, or what we buy, someone is always there doing more, going further, and buying better. **All of this can leave you feeling really discontent.**

My dad often says, "Content people may not have the best of everything, but they make the best of everything." Contentment is being satisfied with what you already have instead of worrying about all the things you don't have.

CONTENT PEOPLE MAY NOT HAVE THE BEST
OF EVERYTHING, BUT THEY MAKE
THE BEST OF EVERYTHING.

Contentment isn't based on an amount of money or how nice your stuff is. Contentment happens on the inside, and when you have it, it doesn't matter how much money you make or how much stuff you have.

When you're not content, you spend your whole life jumping from one thing to another, **always hoping the next thing will be the one big thing that makes you happy.** And, if that's your approach, it will never happen.

The first step toward becoming content is to become grateful. Being grateful requires you to be thankful. **Take the time to express your thankfulness to others.** And when you say "thank you," mean it. Those two words can make a world of difference in helping you become more grateful.

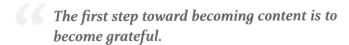
> *The first step toward becoming content is to become grateful.*

Be grateful for what you have instead of focusing so much attention on what you don't have. **Being content with what you have will keep you from spending money you don't have or going into debt for something you don't really need.** And, when you're truly content, you'll find that you really can quit the comparisons with others.

IN A HEART
FILLED WITH
GRATITUDE, THERE
IS NO ROOM FOR
DISCONTENTMENT.

—RACHEL CRUZE

BEING A

JUST A

MILLIONAIRE ISN'T DREAM

MISTAKE 05 // NO MONEY

SAVING MONEY

When I was fourteen years old, I really wanted to have a boom box. They were such a big deal! Almost everyone I knew had one—everyone except me. The only problem was that the model I wanted was almost $150!

My mom and dad said there was no way they were going to spend that much money for me to have loud music in my bedroom. **They told me I could work and save my own money to buy it, though.**

At the time, my parents were giving me about $20 each week for all the things I did around the house. **I tried to save some of that every time I got paid, so in about three months, I had saved the money I needed to buy the boom box.** After the cashier rang it up, I was $3 short because I hadn't figured on the sales tax.

So I went back home and looked everywhere to find some extra money. I found quarters, dimes, nickels, and a lot of pennies in the couch cushions, under my bed, behind my desk, and in some jean pockets.

When I got back to the store, I poured all of the change on to the counter. The cashier watched me as I separated all of the different coins. It was obvious he was annoyed, and he probably wished I had just swiped a card. That would have been easier for him—but I had worked hard to pay with cash.

That was the first purchase that I ever made with money I had earned and saved for a specific reason. It felt good. I didn't know I was teaching myself principles of saving money. I just realized that if I really wanted something, I could save up for it and buy it.

There's a biblical proverb that sums this up: "The wise have wealth and luxury, but fools spend whatever they get" (Proverbs 21:20). This verse encourages me to not spend all of my money as soon as I get it, and instead, to save some.

Out of everything in my bedroom, that boom box always stayed clean. I never put anything on top of it. I made sure it was polished and it always worked. **I took good care of it because I had worked hard for it.**

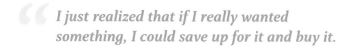

> *I just realized that if I really wanted something, I could save up for it and buy it.*

I kept that boom box for a long time and even took it to college. It was outdated, but I didn't care because it was mine and I bought it with my own hard-earned money.

Saving your money takes discipline, but it's worth it when you can pay cash for your purchases. You'll also take pride in what you buy because you worked hard to save up the money. I make saving a priority by adding it to my budget every month. I've discovered that if I want to have some money, I need to save some money.

NO MONEY

THE BIG FIVE

When it comes to handling your money wisely, you need to have some priorities. While you're in college, you can stick to **The Five Foundations**.

SAVE A $500 EMERGENCY FUND

An emergency fund is money you set aside in a bank savings account to help you cover emergency expenses that may come up, like breaking your phone or computer.

GET OUT OF DEBT

Cut up any credit cards you might have and stay out of debt for life! If you already have debt, throw every dollar you can at it and pay it off as quickly as possible.

PAY CASH FOR YOUR FIRST CAR

Don't take out a car loan or lease a car. Save up and pay cash for a car. That way, you own the car and you don't have to worry about making monthly payments.

PAY CASH FOR COLLEGE

Make it your goal to graduate from college without any school debt. Working, scholarships, and grants can help you pay for college with cash.

04

BUILD WEALTH AND GIVE

It's important to get in the habit of saving and giving away money early in life. Giving will be a tremendous blessing to you and to others!

05

Most people view money simply as a way to get stuff that they want—and they spend it as quickly as they get it. **But to win with money, you need to have a plan.**

The money habits you develop now will impact your financial security and the way you handle money in the future. **The Five Foundations provide the framework for a money plan that will help you win with money!**

NO MONEY

TEN REASONS TO SAVE

Saving money is important. We all know we should save money, but we come up with lots of reasons why we don't. And let's face it: not having money causes lots of stress. In fact, recent surveys indicate that 70% of college students feel stressed about personal finances.[19]

Here are ten reasons you should start saving money now—while you're in college—so you can avoid that money stress:

1. **Money doesn't grow on trees.**
   In order to have money, you need to work and save some of your earnings (unless you have a magic tree).

2. **Cash in the bank feels good.**
   You get a sense of security (and even experience less stress) when you have cash to handle emergencies.

3. **Saving changes you.**
   Saving money builds character by helping you become more responsible and independent.

4. **Car loans are terrible.**
   Set saving goals for purchases like paying cash for a car so you can avoid loans and debt.

5. **Cafeteria food can be awful.**
   You may want to go out to eat and expand your dining options.

6. **College costs a lot.**
   Pay cash for your education instead of using student loans and you may even get a discount.

7. **Weekends require cash.**
   Driving home for a visit, doing laundry, or heading out with friends means you'll need some money.

8. **You'll want to buy stuff.**
   With cash you'll be able to buy clothes and technology without going into debt.

9. **Road trips don't pay for themselves.**
   Hitting the road for spring break or an away game means you'll need to buy gas and snacks.

10. **Driving a car is expensive.**
    From putting gas in the tank to paying for repairs and maintenance, cars are not cheap.

$387

The average cost for a check engine light-related repair:[20]

CASH ON HAND

The question is not *if* an emergency expense will pop up but *when.* Emergencies will happen, and it's always best to have cash on hand to handle them.

The scary reality is that 66 million adults have absolutely no money saved.[21] That's not where you want to find yourself in the event of an emergency. Knowing what to do (saving money) is only going to help you if you actually put what you know into practice—and get some money in the bank.

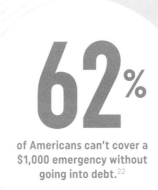

62%
of Americans can't cover a
$1,000 emergency without
going into debt.[22]

PERSONAL FINANCE IS 80% BEHAVIOR AND 20% HEAD KNOWLEDGE

—DAVE RAMSEY

GIVING IS IMPORTANT

You don't have to spend much time on social media before you see a bunch of selfies and other pictures showing how happy everyone appears to be with their lives . . . and their stuff. **With all the focus on self in the world today, it can be tempting to think that life is all about you.** I hate to burst your bubble, but it's not.

Thinking everything is about you can turn you into a selfish person—and let's face it, selfish people aren't much fun to be around. **Here's a great way to become less selfish: become more *selfless* by giving to others.**

When it comes to money, there are three basic things you can do with it: **Spend it, save it, and give it away.**

A good rule of thumb for giving money is 10% of your income. But giving goes way beyond money. If you don't really have much of an income or you're seriously worried about how to pay for your next meal, then find some other ways to give that don't cost anything. **That could mean giving your time or your talents.**

Think about what you have to offer, even if it's not something tangible. **Giving is one of the most important things you can do, so make it a priority!**

WAYS YOU CAN GIVE

This isn't an exhaustive list, but here are some ways you can be a little more selfless by giving to others—and they won't cost you any money:

- » **Volunteer at a homeless shelter.**

- » **Deliver meals to the elderly.**

- » **Visit, sing, or serve at a senior adult care facility.**

- » **Organize an event to raise money for a local charity.**

- » **Volunteer at a food bank or food pantry.**

- » **Wear a fun costume and visit children at a hospital.**

- » **Organize a community cleanup event.**

- » **Volunteer with an after-school program for kids.**

- » **Conduct a shoe or clothing drive for a local charity.**

- » **Volunteer at a local library.**

- » **Coach a youth sports team.**

- » **Volunteer at a local animal shelter.**

- » **Tutor children after school.**

- » **Deliver stuffed animals to a children's hospital.**

SAVE CASH WHILE GETTING CREDITS

Did you know there are several ways you can save on the cost of your tuition? There are. And sometimes you can even earn college credit at the same time.

CLEP TESTS

College-Level Examination Program (CLEP) tests offer you the opportunity to earn a qualifying test score on over thirty college subject tests. That means doing well on a single test could enable you to skip some college courses, which saves you tuition money!

You can find tests in subjects that you may already know quite a bit about. This is a relatively painless way to test out of some college courses—especially prerequisite courses.

The tests typically cost less than $100 to take, so you can earn college credits for a lot less than you would pay per credit hour at your college. Check with your college to see if they accept CLEP tests, what score you would need on the test to receive credit, and how many credit hours you could earn with CLEP testing.

For more information on CLEP testing, check out *clep.collegeboard.org*.

INTERNSHIPS

Internships are another way to earn college credit hours and gain valuable work experience in the process. Don't underestimate the positive way that an internship will look on your résumé.

A paid internship may be hard to find, but earning college credit is the main goal. If you do get paid, use that money to pay for any class costs. Check with your college regarding the guidelines—and any costs—related to internships.

Another benefit of internships is that they allow you to try a career field to find out if it is the right fit for you. For example, if you're interested in medical or nursing school, working in a hospital is a good first step. If you discover that the sight of blood makes you queasy, you've just saved yourself a bunch of time and money.

Internships also connect you with experienced people who can mentor you and give you a great professional reference later. You might even intern for a company that ends up hiring you full time out of college!

PEER LEADERSHIP

As mentioned on page 55, becoming an RA (resident assistant) often comes with free or discounted room and board. This is a fantastic way to trim a huge chunk of your college expenses. However, most schools won't let you become an RA until you've completed your freshman year. Check out the rules at your school.

GIVING MAKES ME
MORE CONSCIOUS
OF THE NEEDS
OF OTHERS. IT
REMINDS ME
THAT LIFE DOESN'T
REVOLVE AROUND
ME AND THAT
EVERYONE NEEDS
EVERYONE ELSE.

—KRISTA P.

LIFE IS EXPENSIVE

Fast-forward to your life after college. It's going to be great! You'll be done with school and won't have to worry about cramming for exams anymore. You'll be working and have plenty of time and money to do whatever you want, right?

Maybe.

It's time for a reality check. Right now, you probably have big plans for your future—including a big income from your dream job. You can't wait to get started!

When I talk with students about their career plans, it's not uncommon for them to think they'll make at least $100,000 a year in their first full-time job out of college. That sure would be nice! But it's not reality for most students.

The average first-job salary for a college graduate is just $37,000 per year.[23] That works out to about $17.75 per hour. That's not bad, but it's a far cry from the money many college students may have their hearts set on.

On the next two pages, **let's take a look at how your income will break down with the real-life expenses you'll have when you graduate**—especially if you buy into society's definition of "normal." Remember, "normal" includes student loan debt, credit card debt, and a car payment.

AVERAGE GRADUATE BUDGET

INCOME

Monthly Income (after taxes) $2,596

EXPENSES

Giving (10%)	$ 260
Rent	$ 600
Utilities	$ 150
Renter's Insurance	$ 20
Cell Phone	$ 75
Groceries	$ 200
Eating Out	$ 150
Entertainment	$ 100
Clothing	$ 100
Car Insurance	$ 230
Gas/Car Repairs	$ 150
Health Insurance	$ 125
Student Loan	$ 444
Credit Card Payment	$ 100
Car Payment	$ 482

TOTAL

Income	$2,596
Expenses	- $3,186

- $590

$37,000 AVG. ANNUAL SALARY

$1,026 MONTHLY DEBT PAYMENTS

GET RID OF DEBT PAYMENTS TO GET A POSITIVE BALANCE.

A WRITTEN PLAN FOR YOUR LIFE

You need to have a written plan for your money. You know that's called a budget. And I've already identified why it's so important to have a plan for your spending and saving.

But it's just as important for you to develop a written plan for your life. Start by setting some goals to work toward. Make sure your goals in life line up with your goals for your money—as reflected in your budget. That way, your money will fuel your goals.

The two written plans—one for your life and one for your money—work together. When you have a written plan for your life and know the goals you want to work toward, it's easier to build a budget for your money that will help you reach your goals.

> *It's important to have both a written plan for your life and a written plan for your money.*

For example, if you say that you want to go to college debt-free, how's your budget reflecting that goal? Are you budgeting money for tuition, books, and food to pay for the next semester without taking out any loans?

If you want to become a millionaire, is that desire reflected in your budget? Are you saving and investing money to help you get there? You won't just wake up one day and be a millionaire. You've got to work toward it.

As you begin your freshman year, write down some goals for the first three months of college. This is going to be a major change from your life in high school, so start simple with goals like:

>> **I'm going to get As and Bs my first semester.**

>> **I'm going to be on time to class every day.**

>> **I'm going to finish all of my assignments on time.**

Start with a few three-month goals. Then write some one-year and three-year goals. The idea is to begin with some short-term goals and then add some long-term ones.

After that, list some goals related to your senior year of college. Keep in mind, at that point, you'll almost be done with your college experience. What job do you want to have? Where can you start interning and building relationships during your junior year?

Finally, think of some goals for after graduation that will carry over into the rest of your life. Of course, your goals will probably change and evolve throughout your time in college, but writing them down now is a great place to start!

When you have your written plan, put it where you will see it at least three times a day. Put a copy on the wall in your dorm room and another one in your class binders. Take a picture and set it as the lock screen on your phone. Make your goals your focus.

Also, make sure to give a copy of your goals to an accountability partner who will check in with you to make sure you stay on track. This person can be a parent, guardian, relative, or a close friend.

When something else comes up to distract you, stay focused on your goals. If you plan to graduate from college debt-free, don't let someone else pressure you into making purchases that will use the money you are saving for school.

Clearly, it's important to have both a written plan for your life and a written plan for your money. They work together to provide you with some basic guidelines to keep your life from getting off track.

As you develop your plan, make sure to identify some ways you will avoid the five mistakes we've addressed in this book. Avoid taking out student loans, stay away from credit cards, make wise choices, live on a budget, and prioritize saving and giving.

I know you can do this. Yes, it's going to take some work. Yes, your friends may give you a hard time. But you can do it! It will be worth it later in your life.

WHEN YOU'RE
TRAVELING
SOMEWHERE
YOU'VE NEVER
BEEN BEFORE, YOU
FIGURE OUT HOW
YOU'RE GOING TO
GET THERE. IN THE
SAME WAY, HAVING
A PLAN FOR YOUR
LIFE WILL GIVE YOU
A CLEAR DIRECTION
TO HEAD IN.

— EMMA B.

RESOURCES

A WRITTEN PLAN FOR MY LIFE

My Favorite Quote:

MY GOALS THIS SEMESTER

Personal Goal:

_____
_____

Things I will do to achieve this goal:

_____
_____
_____

Academic Goal:

_____
_____

Things I will do to achieve this goal:

_____
_____
_____

Financial Goal:

_____
_____

Things I will do to achieve this goal:

_____
_____
_____

TO STAY AWAY FROM THE FIVE MISTAKES, I WILL . . .

1. Avoid Student Loans By:

2. Avoid Buying Stuff on Credit By:

3. Make Smart Choices By:

4. Have a Plan for My Money By:

5. Save Money During College By:

*The caliber of your future depends on
the choices you make today!*

BUDGET FOR THIS MONTH

INCOME

_____ $ _____
_____ $ _____
_____ $ _____

Total = $ _____

EXPENSES

_____ $ _____
_____ $ _____
_____ $ _____
_____ $ _____
_____ $ _____
_____ $ _____
_____ $ _____

Total = $ _____

TOTAL

Income _____ $ _____
Expenses _____ - $ _____

$0

Check out EveryDollar (everydollar.com)
for help with creating a budget.

WANT TO LEARN MORE?

Check out *Foundations in Personal Finance: College Edition* to learn even more about smart money habits. Available in both a five-chapter and twelve-chapter edition.

daveramsey.com/collegestudy

Create your FREE budget in
less than 10 minutes!

EveryDollar.com

NOTES

CHAPTER 1

1. Josh Mitchell, "Student Debt Is About to Set Another Record, But the Picture Isn't All Bad," *The Wall Street Journal*, May 2, 2016, June 3, 2016, http://blogs.wsj.com/economics/2016/05/02/student-debt-is-about-to-set-another-record-but-the-picture-isnt-all-bad/.

2. Trends in Higher Education, "Trends in College Pricing: Average Published Undergraduate Charges by Sector, 2015–16," The College Board, May 3, 2016, https://trends.collegeboard.org/college-pricing/figures-tables/average-published-undergraduate-charges-sector-2015-16.

3. A Public Agenda Report, "With Their Whole Lives Ahead of Them," The Bill and Melinda Gates Foundation, May 3, 2016, http://www.publicagenda.org/pages/with-their-whole-lives-ahead-of-them-reality-1.

CHAPTER 2

4. "Gap Between New and Used Vehicle Payments Widens to Reach an All-Time High," Experian, August 27, 2015, May 16, 2016, http://www.experianplc.com/media/news/2015/q2-2015-safm-pt-2/.

5. "What's in My FICO Scores," myFICO, May 12, 2016, http://www.myfico.com/crediteducation/whatsinyourscore.aspx.

6. Ron Marshall, "How Many Ads Do You See in One Day?" Red Crow Marketing, Inc., September 10, 2015, May 16, 2016, http://www.redcrowmarketing.com/2015/09/10/many-ads-see-one-day/.

7. "How College Students Spend Their Money Infographic," College Owlz, January 19, 2016, May 15, 2016, http://www.collegeowlz.com/blog/2016/01/19/how-college-students-spend-their-money-infographic/.

8. Tamara E. Holmes, "Student Credit, Debit and Prepaid Card Statistics," CreditCards.com, June 15, 2016, June 17, 2016, http://www.creditcards.com/credit-card-news/student-credit-debit-prepaid-statistics.php.

CHAPTER 3

9. "Seven in 10 Americans Seek Out Opinions Before Making Purchases," Mintel, June 3, 2015, June 7, 2016, http://www.mintel.com/press-centre/social-and-lifestyle/seven-in-10-americans-seek-out-opinions-before-making-purchases.

10. Sienna Kossman, "Survey: 5 in 6 Americans Admit to Impulse Buys," CreditCards.com, January 24, 2016, June 9, 2016, http://www.creditcards.com/credit-card-news/impulse-buy-survey.php.

11. "$16 Billion Stolen from 12.7 Million Identity Fraud Victims in 2014," Javelin Strategy & Research, March 3, 2015, June 7, 2016, http://www.javelinstrategy.

com/press-release/16-billion-stolen-127-million-identity-fraud-victims-2014-according-javelin-strategy.

12. "What's the Price Tag for a College Education?" COLLEGEdata, June 1, 2016, http://www.collegedata.com/cs/content/content_payarticle_tmpl.jhtml?articleId=10064.

13. Ibid.

14. Dan Kopf, "Which Major Has the Most Expensive Textbooks?" Priceonomics, August 24, 2015, November 7, 2016, http://priceonomics.com/which-major-has-the-most-expensive-textbooks.

15. Liana Solis, "Expert Analyzes Students' Netflix Usage," Daily Toreador, October 14, 2014, November 15, 2016, http://www.dailytoreador.com/lavida/expert-analyzes-students-netflix-usage/article_0dfc194a-5412-11e4-9415-001a4bcf6878.html.

CHAPTER 4

16. Dennis Jacobe, "One in Three Americans Prepare a Detailed Household Budget," Gallup, June 3, 2013, June 27, 2016, http://www.gallup.com/poll/162872/one-three-americans-prepare-detailed-household-budget.aspx.

17. "The Cost of an Average Date," Phillips & Company, March 29, 2016, July 1, 2016, http://y98.cbslocal.com/2016/03/29/the-cost-of-an-average-date/.

18. "Seventy Percent of College Students Work While Enrolled," Georgetown University Center on Education and the Workforce, October 28, 2015, July 7, 2016, https://cew.georgetown.edu/wp-content/uploads/Press-release-WorkingLearners__FINAL.pdf.

CHAPTER 5

19. Jeff Grabmeier, "70 Percent of College Students Stressed About Finances," The Ohio State University, July 1, 2015, July 27, 2016, https://news.osu.edu/news/2015/07/01/financial-wellness/.

20. "2016 State Repair Cost Rankings," CarMD, June 2016, July 8, 2016, https://www.carmd.com/wp/vehicle-health-index-introduction/2016-carmd-state-index/.

21. Jessica Dickler, "66 Million of Us Have No Emergency Savings," USA Today, June 25, 2016, August 17, 2016, http://www.usatoday.com/story/money/personalfinance/2016/06/25/66-million-us-have-no-emergency-savings/85990074/.

22. Claes Bell, "Budgets Can Crumble in Times of Trouble," Bankrate, January 7, 2015, September 14, 2016, http://www.bankrate.com/finance/smart-spending/money-pulse-0115.aspx.

23. Alyssa Davis, Will Kimball, and Elise Gould, "The Class of 2015: Despite an Improving Economy, Young Grads Still Face an Uphill Climb," Economic Policy Institute, May 27, 2015, September 18, 2016, http://www.epi.org/publication/the-class-of-2015/#epi-toc-9.

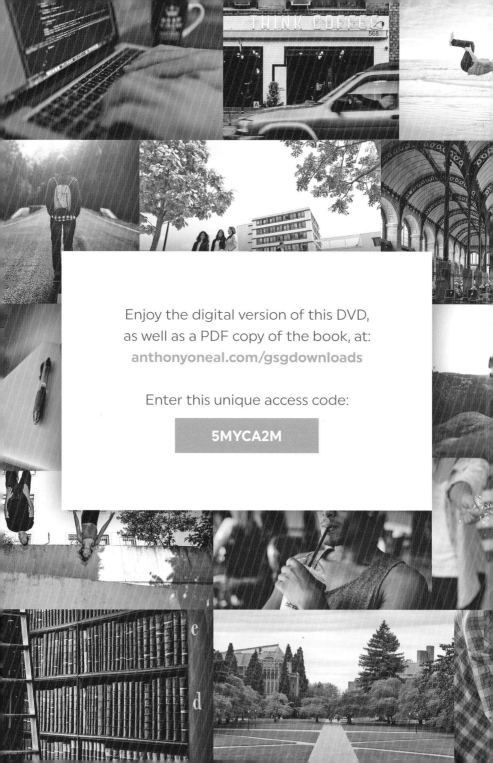

Enjoy the digital version of this DVD,
as well as a PDF copy of the book, at:

anthonyoneal.com/gsgdownloads

Enter this unique access code:

5MYCA2M